Oh, The Things I Can Be When I See Me

By

Valerie J. Lewis Coleman

Published by

Pen of the Writer, LLC
Englewood, OH
PenOfTheWriter.com

Pen of the Writer, LLC
Englewood, OH
PenOfTheWriter.com

Copyright © 2019 by Valerie J. Lewis Coleman,
Samara Lewis and Lyric Lewis

All rights reserved. No part of this book may be reproduced or transmitted in any form or by any means, electronic or mechanical, without prior written consent of the author, except for brief quotes in a review.

Library of Congress Control Number: 2019908216

ISBN-13: 978-0-9786066-8-8

Cover design and illustrations by Natasza Remesz

Edited by Tenita C. Johnson

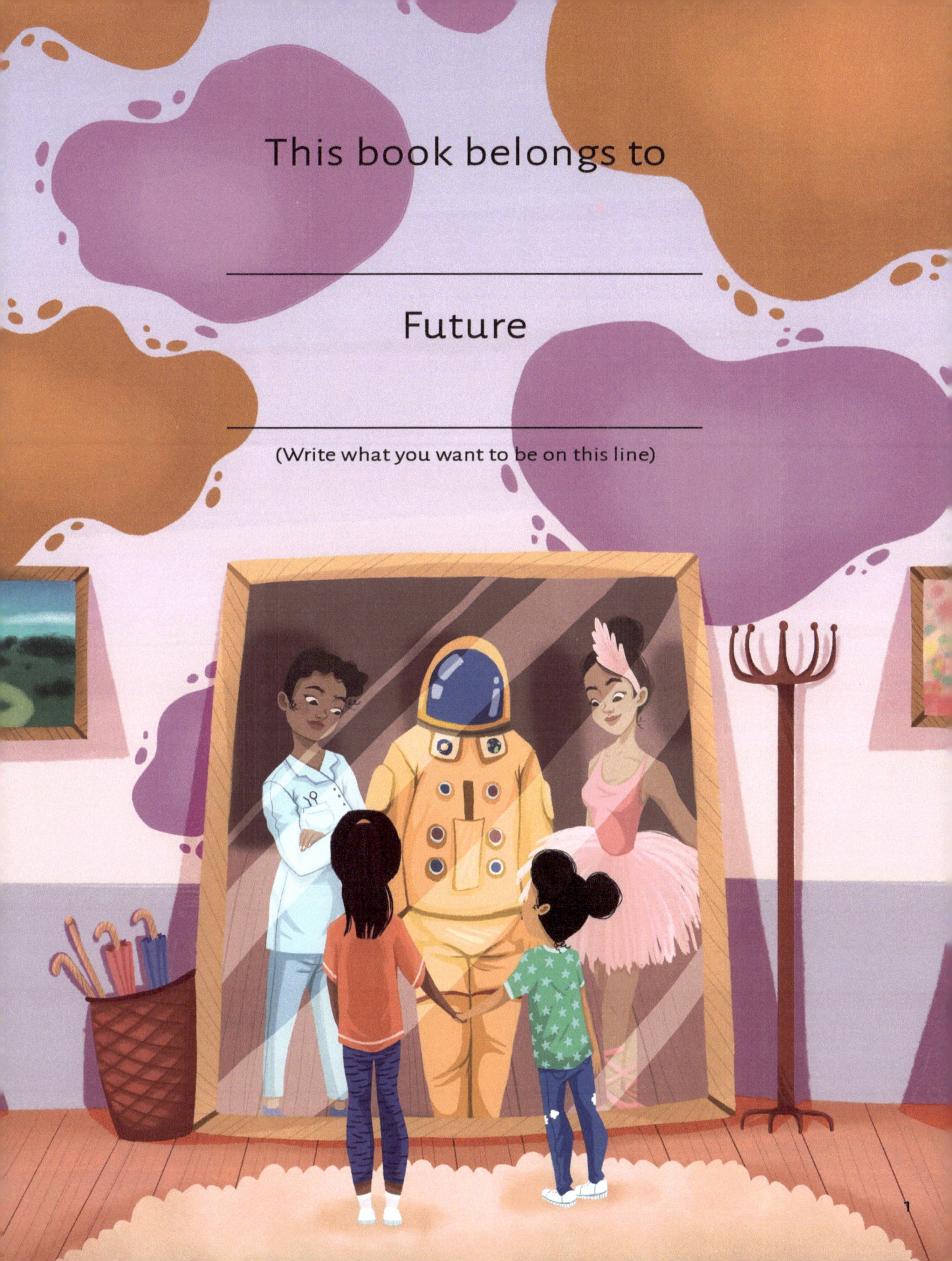

Samara and Lyric are cousins. They love to visit their grandmother, MeMe.

"I am so glad you are here," MeMe said while hugging her grandbabies. "What do you want to do first?"

"Paint!" Samara jumped three times.

MeMe laughed. "Okay, Samara. Let's paint." She took Lyric by the hand.

Samara said, "MeMe, I love creativity because I can make what I see in my mind."

"That's visual art. You can tell a story using photos like Lorna Simpson, sculptures like Simone Leigh or quilts like Faith Ringgold. Artists like Zora Neale Hurston, Maya Angelou and Vanessa Miller Pierce wrote books, plays and movie scripts."

Lyric said, "My favorite colors are orange, blue and green." She looked up from her artwork. "Do you like it, MeMe?"

"Yes! Such beautiful masterpieces. Let's get you cleaned up while your paintings dry."

"Since you two love to perform, you can be artists who dance, sing or play instruments. Katherine Dunham formed one of the first Negro ballet companies in America. She toured the world and danced in several movies."

Samara said, "Did you dance with her?"

MeMe laughed. "No, baby. She opened the school in 1930 long before MeMe was born." She rubbed Samara's back. "You saw Disney's *The NutCracker and the Four Realms*, right?"

Samara nodded.

"The ballerina, Misty Copeland, is the first black female principal dancer for the American Ballet Theatre."

Lyric said, "MeMe, look at me! I'm a ballerina."

"Do it, baby!"

Lyric stumbled.

MeMe helped her balance. "Let's sing for a while. This art form has many great examples. Nina Simone sang black classical music, Leontyne Price sang opera and Minnie Riperton —"

"MeMe, I haven't heard their songs."

"Probably not, Samara. What about Mariah Carey, Jennifer Hudson or Tonya Baker?"

"Yes! I will do it all like Zendaya. She dances, sings and acts."

They sang, "Oh, the things I can be when I see me."

Lyric picked up her toy guitar and put on her fancy glasses.

MeMe said, "Lyric, a musician is another type of performing artist. Sister Rosetta Tharpe made her career as a gospel guitarist. She played with Cab Calloway at Harlem's Cotton Club."

Samara plinked her piano and sang *Lost Boy*.

MeMe laughed. "So you want to sing and play like Ruth B. ?"

"Yes, ma'am."

"I love it! With enough practice, you can do two-piano performances like Hazel Scott and Alicia Keys." She looked at the clock. "It's time to meet your cousin at the park. Let's get out of those tutus."

The family walked to the park to meet MeMe's other granddaughter whose nickname is Yaya.

MeMe said, "Samara, do you still want to be a gymnast?"

"Yes, ma'am."

"Then let me see what you've got."

Yaya walked toward MeMe. She hugged her grandmother and then played with her cousins.

Samara said, "I'm Simone Biles!"

Yaya said, "I'm Gabby Douglas!"

"You ladies still have plenty of energy. How about a race?"

Samara and Yaya said, "Yeah!"

"Give Lyric a head start." MeMe helped Lyric. "Did you know I ran track in high school?"

"You want to race with us," Yaya asked.

"No thanks." MeMe smiled. "My classmate, LaVonna Martin-Floreal, won a silver medal in the 1992 Olympics."

"Wow. She's fast," Samara said as she readied to race.

"She sure was. She outran everyone in school. She wanted you to know that being a winner means working hard and having fun."

"Really?"

"Uh huh. In the 1960 Olympics, Wilma Rudolph won three gold medals and broke several world records."

Yaya said, "Did you race her?"

MeMe shook her head. "Serena Williams is an amazing athlete, too. She's been the No. 1 tennis player in the world several times. Althea Gibson helped make that possible as the first great African-American player in women's tennis."

Samara said, "Who's your favorite soccer player?"

Lyric said, "Charisse!"

MeMe smiled. "Your cousin counts. She's my favorite, too." MeMe looked toward the parking lot. "Yaya's mother is here. Give her hugs and kisses."

The family walked home to prepare for bed.

"Good morning." MeMe kissed her grandbabies.

"Good morning, MeMe."

"Yesterday, you were artists, dancers and athletes. What do you want to be today?"

Lyric rubbed her eyes. "I want to be an actress."

Samara stretched, "I want to direct!"

MeMe said, "What's your favorite movie?"

The girls shouted, "*Black Panther*!"

"As an actress, you can be a queen like Angela Bassett, a scientist like Letitia Wright or a secret agent like Lupita Nyong'o."

Lyric struck a pose.

Samara grabbed her tablet. "And…scene!"

"Ava DuVernay directs movies with people who look like you including *A Wrinkle in Time*."

Samara said, "MeMe, who is your favorite actress?"

"Hmmm, my favorite actors are Denzel Washington and Bryant Louis Bentley. But actress?" MeMe tapped her chin. "Cicely Tyson, Regina King, Tracee Ellis Ross and the little girl from *Blackish*, Marsai Martin."

"Why Marsai?"

"She is the youngest producer in Hollywood at fourteen years old."

Michelle Obama appeared on the TV screen.

MeMe said, "Samara, what can you tell me about Michelle Obama?"

"She was First Lady of the United States for eight years."

"Very good. Did you know that she went to two Ivy League schools and was an amazing attorney before she lived in the White House?"

"No, ma'am. What do attorneys do?"

"Judges and attorneys make sure everyone is treated fairly. Judges Lynn Toler and Faith Jenkins have TV shows helping people solve tough problems."

"Do you know any *real* attorneys?"

"All of them are real. Are you asking if I personally know some?"

"Yes, ma'am."

"Your Aunty Deena and Cousin Aisha are both attorneys. Maybe you can spend a day with them at work to learn how they help people."

"I'd like that."

"Samara, what's your favorite subject in school?"

"Reading!"

Lyric said, "I love reading, too."

"You can learn so much reading. MeMe learned how to be an engineer by reading and loving math. You can be a scientist, inventor or mathematician. Dr. Gladys West was the woman behind GPS technology."

Samara shrugged.

"You know, recalculating route."

Samara smiled. "I want to invent an app for girls."

"Absolutely. Judy Jordan-Brunson, MeMe's college friend, is a top executive in the automotive industry. She has several patents for her inventions. Raye Montague was an engineer who designed ships for the U.S. Navy and Katherine Johnson used math to get astronauts to the moon. Taraji P. Henson did a great job acting as Ms. Johnson in *Hidden Figures*."

Lyric said, "MeMe, I want to be an astronaut on the moon."

"You can do it! Dr. Mae Jemison was the first African-American woman in space. She loved school so much that she has degrees in chemical engineering, Afro-American studies and medicine."

"Wow." Samara's eyes were opened wide.

"And she speaks several languages. How many languages can you speak, Samara?"

"I know some Spanish and little brother. Shawn has his own language."

"You're funny."

Lyric held up three fingers. "Uno, dos, tres."

"Very good, Lyric," MeMe nodded and smiled. "Do you still want to be a baby doctor?"

"No, I want to be a dog doctor."

"You can be whatever kind of doctor you want."

"Dr. Danielle Spencer was a child actress on the TV show *What's Happening*. She became a veterinarian taking care of animals. Dr. Tanisha Richmond is a foot doctor and Dr. Rosalind Jackson is a medical doctor for women. She delivers babies and helps MeMe feel better."

"MeMe, does your pumach hurt," Lyric asked, rubbing MeMe's stomach.

"I'm fine, precious." She kissed Lyric on the top of her head. "MeMe's friend, Karen Townsend, is also a doctor, but she doesn't have patients. She has clients who hire her to show them how to work together."

Samara put on one of MeMe's dresses.

MeMe said, "What are you doing?"

"I'm Madam C.J. Walker."

"What do you know about her?"

"She was the first American woman to become a self-made millionaire."

"Okay, Samara. You're so smart. Madam C.J. Walker made her fortune helping us take care of our hair."

"My mommy takes care of my hair," Lyric said, tugging at an afro puff.

"Yes, she does." MeMe hugged Lyric. "An entrepreneur owns their own company."

Samara said, "Like you?"

"Yes, baby. People hire your MeMe to write, publish and market bestselling books. Darnyelle Jervey Harmon coaches businesswomen and Lynnette Khalfani Cox helps people with their money. My friend, Linda J. Hawkins, shows women how to eat and live healthy. Can you think of any other businesswomen?"

Samara said, "Oprah Winfrey and my mom."

"Very good." MeMe smiled. "Mikaila Ulmer owns Bee Sweet Lemonade and Alianna Hines was nine years old when she started buying and selling houses."

"I can be a business owner now?"

"Absolutely. Anything you love to do—and do well—can be your business."

"MeMe, can we play outside," Lyric asked, pulling MeMe's robe.

"Yes, baby. Let's get your play clothes."

Lyric crawled on the ground. "I want to be a police officer and a firefighter."

"It makes me happy to know that you want to help people. Annette Nance-Holt is the first woman to be deputy fire commissioner in Chicago. She is responsible for the safety of millions of people. Guess what."

Lyric stopped playing. "What?"

"She asked me to tell you 'never give up and don't let anyone tell you that you can't do it.'"

Lyric smiled. "Sparky said, 'Get low and go!'"

"You smell like outside. Let's freshen up before lunch."

MeMe and her babies went in the kitchen.

MeMe said, "Samara, what's your favorite food?"

"MeMe's mac and cheese and cabbage!" She paused. "And sushi."

"Aw, thank you, baby. I got the recipes from my mom, MeMa." She kissed Samara's cheek. "Lyric, what foods do you like?"

"Pupcakes!"

"Pupcakes it is, my love. Chef Avanelle James would be pleased to know you like to make pastries."

Samara said, "MeMe, who's your favorite chef?"

"Good question. I like several chefs because they use their talent to help others. Elle Simone Scott uses her skills to teach women how to cook. Samantha Davis and Tirzah Love focus on healthy lifestyles with food."

"That's important," Samara said as she stirred the batter.

"Yes, it is. Ayesha Curry works to make sure kids have food to eat. I've been to Sylvia Woods' restaurant in Harlem several times. The food was great and so was the band."

"Can we go to her restaurant?"

"We sure can. Until then, your parents can buy some of her food in the grocery store."

After eating the yummy cupcakes, MeMe said, "Your fathers will be here soon. Do you have anything else you want to be?"

Samara said, "I want to be a teacher so I can help students learn." She ran into the family room to get ready for class.

MeMe and Lyric joined her.

MeMe said, "Who are your students?"

"Adalynn, Lexi, Jade and Noah."

MeMe smiled. "It's Lyric's turn to teach."

Lyric said, "I am Ms. Sonia. MeMe, you are Ms. Pie."

"Yes, ma'am. And who are your students?"

"Carter, Ashley, Samaria, Josiah, Olivia, Madison and Grace."

"Looks like we need to get more toys, I mean students."

Lyric said, "MeMe, I want to be an archaeologist."

"What do you know about archaeologists?"

"Ms. Pie told me that they find dinosaur bones."

"That's a big word for such a little girl. Good for you. When you find a new dinosaur, you can name it Lyric-a-saurus."

Lyric smiled.

The doorbell chimed.

"Okay, MeMe's princesses. Your fathers are here."

The girls hugged and kissed their grandmother.

"Let me see your princess wave. Wrist, wrist, elbow, elbow."

The girls sang, "Oh, the things I can be when I see me!"

"Oh, the things I can

What do you want to be when you grow up?

Why?

Who has already done it?

How did they do it?

What do you need to do to do it?

Who can help you?

Oh, The Things I Can Be When I See Me Seek-and-Find

Everywhere you look, you can see examples of powerful women doing amazing things.

You can be whatever you want to be, too!

As you find the careers in the puzzle, think about the women mentioned in

Oh, The Things I Can Be When I See Me.

```
D A R C H A E O L O G I S T
I F I R E F I G H T E R I B
R L A S T R O N A U T A N A
E A C H E F J U D G E T G L
C W T D I A U T H O R H E L
T Y R M U S I C I A N L R E
O E E T E A C H E R C E Q R
R R S C I E N T I S T T V I
B U S I N E S S O W N E R N
E N G I N E E R T S I T R A
P O L I C E O F F I C E R X
I N V E N T O R D O C T O R
```

Actress	Business Owner	Inventor
Astronaut	Chef	Judge
Archaeologist	Director	Lawyer
Artist	Doctor	Musician
Athlete	Engineer	Scientist
Author	Fire Fighter	Singer
Ballerina	Police Officer	Teacher

Visual Artists
Simone Leigh SimoneLeigh.com
Faith Ringgold FaithRinggold.com
Lorna Simpson LSimpsonStudio.com

Literary Artists
Maya Angelou MayaAngelou.com
Zora Neale Hurston ZoraNealeHurston.com
Vanessa Miller Pierce VanessaMiller.com

Dancers
Misty Copeland MistyCopeland.com
Katherine Dunham KDCAH.org

Singers
Tonya Baker TonyaBakerMinistries.org
Mariah Carey MariahCarey.com
Jennifer Hudson JenniferHudsonOnline.com
Nina Simone NinaSimone.com
Zendaya Zendaya.com

Musicians
Alicia Keys AliciaKeys.com

Athletes
Simone Biles SimoneBiles.com
Gabby Douglas GabrielleDouglas.com
Serena Williams SerenaWilliams.com

Directors
Ava DuVernay AvaDuVernay.com

Attorneys and Judges
Faith Jenkins JudgeFaith.com
Michelle Obama Obama.org
Lynn Toler JudgeLynn.com
Deena Wingard YourReasonableService.net

Doctors
Dr. Rosalind Jackson DrRozMD.com
Dr. Tanisha Richmond RichFeet.org
Dr. Danielle Spencer-David DanielleSpencerWorld.com
Dr. Karen M. R. Townsend DrKarenTownsend.com

Businesswomen
Valerie J. Lewis Coleman PenOfTheWriter.com
Darnyelle Jervey Harmon IncredibleOneEnterprises.com
Linda J. Hawkins SavvyHealthCoaching.com
Alianna Hines AliannaHines.com
Lynnette Khalfani-Cox TheMoneyCoach.net
Mikaila Ulmer MeAndTheBees.com
Madam C.J. Walker MadamCJWalker.com
Oprah Winfrey Oprah.com

Chefs and Bakers
Ayesha Curry AyeshaCurry.com
Samantha Davis SavorBySam.com
Tirzah Love TirzahCatering.com
Sylvia Woods SylviasRestaurant.com

Valerie is available to speak to your girls about career opportunities and setting goals to achieve them. Connect with her at info@penofthewriter.com or 888.802.1802.

For bulk purchases of Oh, The Things I Can Be When I See Me, multicultural crayons and complimentary coloring sketches, visit ThingsICanBe.com.

www.ingramcontent.com/pod-product-compliance
Lightning Source LLC
Chambersburg PA
CBHW041119300426
44112CB00002B/37